Daniel and the Lions

written and illustrated by Heidi Petach

This Bible story is found in Daniel 6.

Fourth Printing, 1991
Library of Congress Catalog Card No. 83-051636

Darius the Mede was king over all the land.

He chose 120 princes to rule under him.
Then he chose three presidents to rule the
princes.

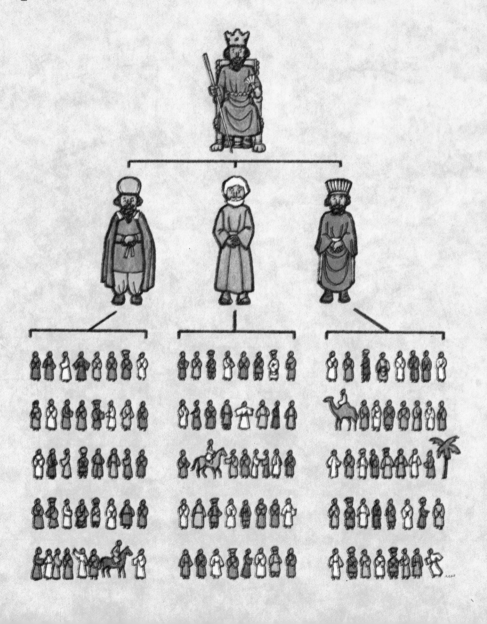

Daniel was one of the presidents. King Darius liked Daniel the best because he was honest and did what was right.

All the other rulers were jealous of Daniel.

They decided to catch him in a mistake. But no one could find anything wrong. Daniel always worked hard, and he always did a good job.

"There is only one way we can get Daniel," one of the princes said. "Listen! I have a plan. . . ."

Daniel's enemies went to see King Darius. "O King," they said, "we think you should make a law that says for thirty days no

one may pray to any god or man except you. Anyone who breaks this law will be thrown into the lions' den."

"Sign here, Sire. Now it is a law of the Medes and Persians. It can never be changed!"

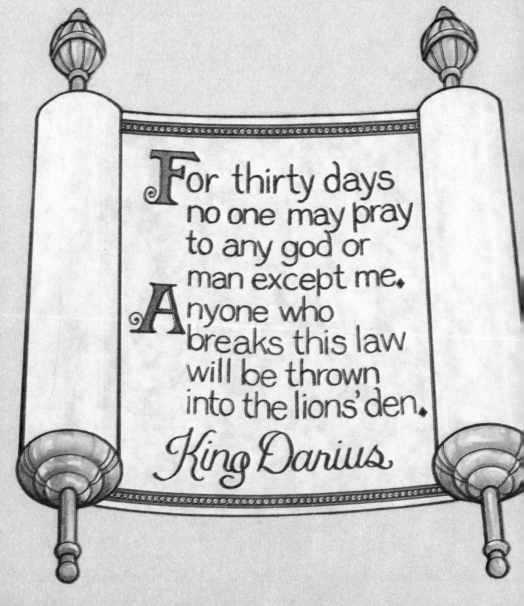

For thirty days no one may pray to any god or man except me. Anyone who breaks this law will be thrown into the lions' den. King Darius

On top of Daniel's house was a room. He liked praying to God there.

Daniel knew about the new law. But God came first. Three times every day Daniel knelt and prayed to God.

"Aha!" cried Daniel's enemies. They had been watching. They ran to the king.

"Daniel has broken your new law!" they said. "He must be thrown to the lions!"

The king was very upset. He liked Daniel.
He tried all day to find a way to change the
law.

At the end of the day Daniel's enemies came back. "You know, O king, that the law of the Medes and Persians can never be changed."

King Darius had to call for Daniel. "May your God, whom you serve so well, save you," he said.

The lions were roaring for their dinner.
Soldiers threw Daniel down into the dark
den.

They put a big stone over the door and poured hot wax around it. The king pressed his signet ring in the wax so no one would open the door.

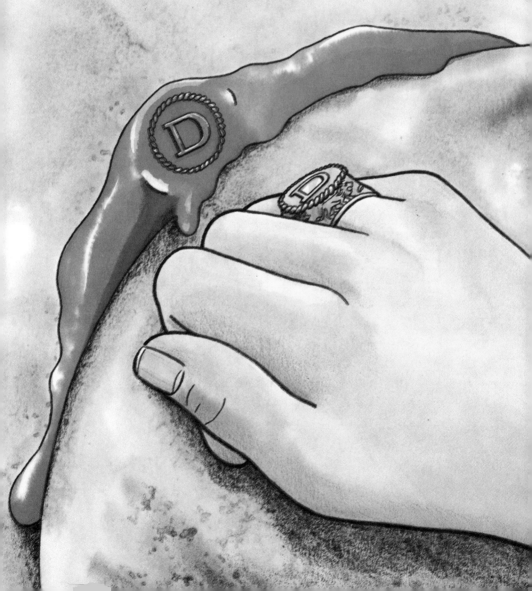

King Darius felt terrible. He didn't want any dinner or music. He worried about Daniel all night.

Finally the sun came up. The king ran to the lions' den. Was Daniel still alive? "Daniel!" he called, "has your God saved you?"

The king was very happy. So were the lions. The men who were Daniel's enemies were tossed into the lions' den and the lions ate them for breakfast.

Then King Darius made a new law. It said, "Everyone must worship Daniel's God, for He is the living God. He saved Daniel from being killed in the lions' den."